Complete
Writing Lessons

For The Primary Grades

by Marjorie Frank

Illustrated by Kathleen Bullock

Illustrations and cover design by Kathleen Bullock
Edited by Sally D. Sharpe

ISBN 0-86530-163-8

Contents

Before You Use This Book

For 15 years I've been listening to teachers talk about writing. I've learned that they're hungry for exciting writing activities. They want loads of great motivators that will help students start writing.

However, teachers are just as interested in the entire writing process. In fact, more than anything else, teachers ask for help with the steps that follow the great motivating activity. They want to know:

- how to get their students to gather raw material
- how to get kids through the painful "rough draft" stage
- how to get young writers to organize ideas and give form to the written piece
- how to get kids to criticize and polish their own (and others') writing
- how to work on different kinds of writing skills (which ones to work on and when)
- how to evaluate finished products and what to do with them

I wrote IF YOU'RE TRYING TO TEACH KIDS HOW TO WRITE, YOU'VE GOTTA HAVE THIS BOOK! because I believe that teachers must include both the fun activities that stimulate writing and the "heavier" skills that include organizing, refining, and editing. I still believe that. Now, however, teachers want more than ideas or an outline of the writing process. They want actual lessons -- from start to finish. Ideas are easy to come by, but complete directions for implementing ideas are not as easy to find.

COMPLETE WRITING LESSONS FOR THE PRIMARY GRADES is what teachers have requested. Each lesson begins with a high-interest activity that will motivate writers. Then the lesson shows you, the teacher, how to help students collect and organize ideas, write a rough draft, criticize and revise written material, work on specific writing skills, and share the finished product.

These lessons are just the beginning. Once you've used them, you'll be able to create your own. By choosing a topic that sparks the interest of your students and by following the format used in this book, you can turn a topic into a complete writing experience. By the time you've finished this book, you will have grown as much as your writers!

Marjorie Frank

How To Use The Lessons

The major premise of this book is this: *students learn the writing process best through teacher-directed writing sessions.*

This doesn't mean that kids shouldn't write on their own. Even young writers love to keep diaries, work in writing centers, and work on independent projects. However, kids do not learn the writing process effectively unless someone teaches it to them, step by step. Once students know the process, they are able to write on their own more successfully.

This is why the activities in this book have been created as teacher-directed lessons. The lessons, four pages each (with the exception of the last lesson of two pages), contain the following elements:

Pages 1 & 2:
> *Teacher Lesson Plan* pages. These pages explain how to guide writers through each step of the writing process as outlined in each activity. (This process is explained on pages 6 and 7.)

Pages 3 & 4:
> *Student Pages** and/or *Example Pages**.
> In every lesson you will find one or two pages designed for students to use in one stage of the writing process. These pages are not meant to be given out as independent writing assignments, but are to be used as a part of a teacher-directed lesson.
>
> Most lessons contain one page of examples.
> The examples illustrate some of the finished products that may result from the lesson.
>
> The examples can also serve as motivators for students. Read the examples aloud to get students excited about a topic and to show them possibilities for writing.

*   You have permission to reproduce any of the student or example pages in quantities sufficient for your students.

The Writing Process

Each lesson in this book includes these steps:

Romancing

This step describes a specific activity, discussion, piece of literature, or situation that will get students excited about a writing form or an idea. (Be sure to spend plenty of time on this stage.) When kids don't want to write or can't think of anything to say, they usually haven't been "romanced" enough.

Collecting

This step is also a "romantic" stage. Collecting is the most fun and creative part of the writing process. Each lesson gives questions to ask, directions to give, and suggestions to make which will start ideas flowing and will help writers gather phrases, words and thoughts to use as "raw material". This step goes fast, so collect plenty of ideas. (You don't have to use all of the ideas, but you may choose from the assortment.)

Writing

This step will give you precise instructions and questions which will direct writers as they choose, organize, and combine "raw material" into a written piece.

Praising

This is a crucial step in the "criticism" stage. This is the stage in which good writing techniques are reinforced. The positive "judging" of a written piece should not be omitted. Each lesson plan gives specific directions as to what you can say to help students see the strengths of their writing. In this stage you will teach your writers to search for examples of good writing skills and to compliment one another on them. For example:

"The phrase 'slippery, slinky snake' made me feel that I was actually touching a snake!"

"You chose wonderful 'wet' words for this rain poem such as slush, drizzle, slurp, and soggy."

"The opening word 'Crash!' really grabbed my interest."

Polishing

This step will tell you what to do, say, and ask to get writers reorganizing, refining, and rewriting their pieces. One or two specific editing skills will be emphasized in each lesson. You can also teach kids to ask questions and make suggestions that are helpful to other writers. For example:

"It seems these two sentences say the same thing."

"The word pretty is used so often. How about using 'lovely' instead?"

"I think this idea might fit better in the next paragraph."

"I'd like to know more about the kitten. Could you add one more sentence?"

Showing Off

You give purpose and dignity to a piece of writing when you provide a way for writers to share what they've written. Each lesson suggests one or more ways to "show off" the students' writing.

NOTE:

Be sure to instruct students to check and correct grammar, spelling, and mechanics at the "polishing" stage.

Writing Skills Checklist

_____ Using words that readers can understand

_____ Substituting stronger words (more colorful, more specific)

_____ Including active words

_____ Rearranging words within a sentence

_____ Rearranging words for clarity

_____ Including more detail

_____ Choosing complementary words and phrases

_____ Using examples

_____ Rearranging sentences for more clarity

_____ Rearranging sentences for better sound

_____ Making strong endings

_____ Creating exciting beginnings

_____ Adding details

_____ Eliminating repetitive ideas or sentences

_____ Eliminating unnecessary ideas or sentences

_____ Eliminating long sentences

_____ Rearranging sentences for better sequence

_____ Adding words and phrases that create a certain mood

_____ Varying sentences (statements, exclamations, questions, compound sentences)

_____ Using metaphors and similes

_____ Using ideas with which readers can identify

_____ Creating simple rhymes

_____ Creating interesting and appropriate titles

1. Alpha-bits

Materials
- drawing paper and colored construction paper
- scissors, glue, markers (or crayons or paints)
- dictionaries (student level)

Romancing
- Read aloud Lilian Obligado's FAINT FROGS FEELING FEVERISH (The Viking Press) or some of the examples from page 13.
- Give the students time to illustrate one of the examples (optional).
- Have the class sit in a circle. Start a word game by saying the word monkey. Tell the students that you are going to "pass" the word around the circle, and that each student should try to add a word which begins with m. When four or five words have been added, start a new phrase which begins with another letter of the alphabet.

Collecting
- Let the class choose one letter of the alphabet.
- Begin building some lists of things, actions, and descriptive words that begin with the chosen letter. (The students may use dictionaries.)
- Create some fun, alliterative phrases as a class. Write the phrases on the board.
- Give each student a copy of the student page "Alphabet Soup" (page 12). Working alone or in pairs, have the students choose one letter of the alphabet and collect words beginning with that letter. (Encourage students to choose different letters so that the whole alphabet is covered.)

Writing
- When the students have a good collection of words, help them combine the words into phrases. The students may write as many phrases for one letter as they would like.

Praising
- Point out interesting or funny phrases.
- Look for phrases that sound especially pleasing such as "popping purple popcorn".

Polishing
- Have the students try to add other words to their phrases.
- Instruct the students to replace inactive words with active ones.
- Tell the students to rearrange words to make the phrases sound better.

Showing Off
- Have each student choose one polished phrase and make an illustration of the phrase using crayons, markers, torn paper or paint.
- The students should neatly print or write their phrases in ink or marker on their illustrations (large enough to be easily read).
- Bind the illustrated phrases into a class book titled "Alphabet Soup". Form a committee to collect the pages, assemble the book, and create a cover.

Baby Bears Blowing Bubbles

Alphabet Soup

I choose the letter _____ .

List *things, people* or *places* that begin with this letter.

_____

_____

_____

List *action words* that begin with this letter.

_____

_____

_____

_____

List *descriptive words* that begin with this letter.

_____

_____

_____

_____

Fred's favorite frog

Which witch washes windows?

dandelions dizzily dancing

More Examples:

Carol's crumbling cookies
mischievous monsters making music
three thieves thinking
elephants eagerly eating eggplants
lobsters licking lemon lollipops
pink panthers popping popcorn
juggling joggers jumping
jack-o'-lanterns
baby bears blowing bubbles

13

2. High-Flying Metaphors

Materials
- typing paper, pencils
- markers and/or crayons

Romancing
- Give each student a copy of the student page "Make Your Own Airplane" (page 17), and help the students follow the directions to make their own planes.
- Take the class outside and let them fly their planes.
- Let the class talk about their experiences with the planes.

Collecting
- Have the class make lists of words and phrases that describe the planes. For example:

how high they fly	sounds they make
actions, movements	how they fall and crash

- Help the students make comparisons between their planes and other things that fly, swoop, crash and glide. Write the comparisons on the board.

Writing
1) Give each student a copy of the student page "Once Upon An Airplane" (page 16). Have the class review the list of ideas collected.
2) Have the students complete page 16 using collected words, similes, phrases, and ideas of their own.

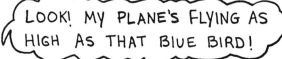

LOOK! MY PLANE'S FLYING AS HIGH AS THAT BLUE BIRD!

FREE-FLOATING FLYER

Praising
- Point out unusual and interesting comparisons.
- Look for words that describe actions, sounds and phrases that capture the "feel" of flying.

Polishing
- Instruct the students to give their phrases variety by eliminating those that are too much alike.
- Ask the students to add two or three good "sound" words to their phrases.
- Have the students eliminate overused metaphors. Help the students brainstorm for fresh, interesting metaphors.

Showing Off
- Have each student write five metaphors on his or her airplane with a marker.
- Have the students decorate their planes with bright colors.
- Hang the airplanes from the classroom ceiling with string.

Once Upon An Airplane

My airplane flies as high as _____

or _____ .

My airplane flies as fast as _____ .

It swoops and loops like _____ .

It swishes through the air faster than _____

_____ .

My airplane sounds like _____

or _____

_____ .

It crashes to the ground like _____ .

It reminds me of _____

or a _____ .

My airplane is a _____

or a _____ .

Choose five of your favorite metaphors to write on your airplane.

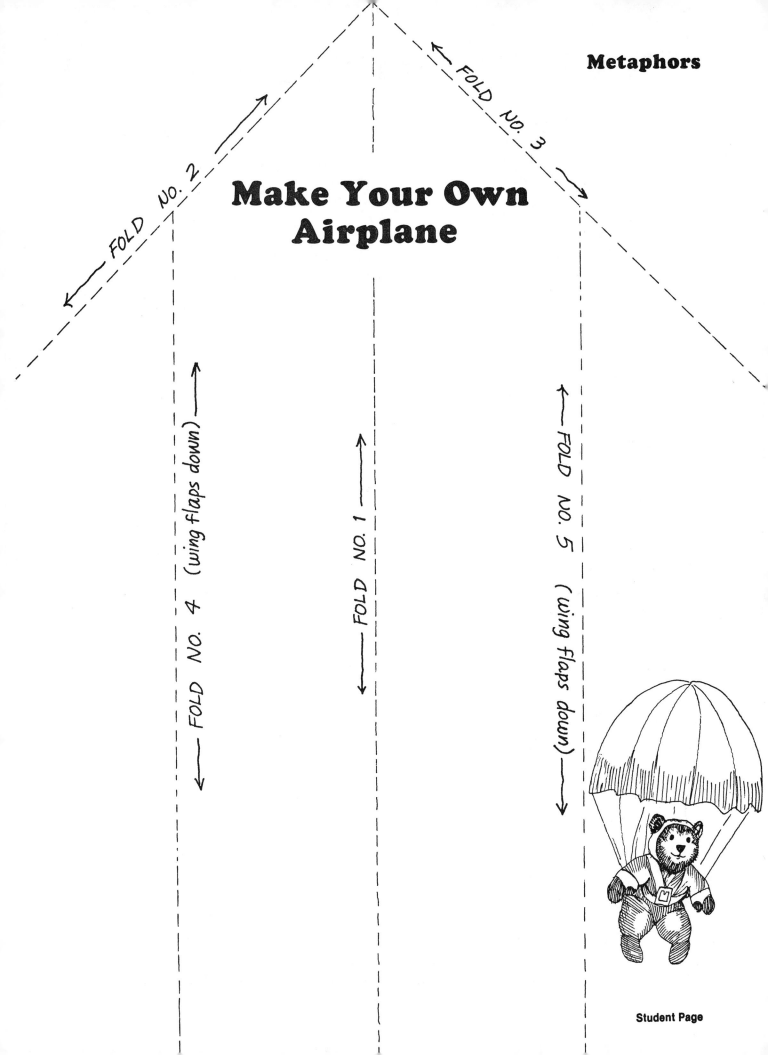

Metaphors

FOLD NO. 3

FOLD NO. 2

Make Your Own
Airplane

FOLD NO. 4 (wing flaps down)

FOLD NO. 1

FOLD NO. 5 (wing flaps down)

Student Page

3. It's Raining! It's Pouring!

Materials
- blue poster board, scissors, markers, glue
- clothespins
- large umbrella
- poems and songs about rain (Peter Spier's RAIN)

Romancing
- The best catalyst for "rain" writing is a wet, rainy day. On a rainy day, the class can really hear, feel, smell, taste, and enjoy the rain. Even if it's not raining, reading books and poems and singing songs about rain will set the mood for "rain" writing.
- Have the class talk about experiences they've had in rainstorms.

Collecting
- Help the students brainstorm a list of "wet" words and phrases by asking them these questions:

  Can you think of some words that make you feel wet?
  What sound does the rain make?
  What does the air smell like during a rain?
  What does rain look like?
  What are some things that rain does?
  What do you do in the rain?

- As the class brainstorms, write the words and phrases on the board.

18

Writing

1) Give each student a copy of the student page "A Slushy, Sloppy Day" (page 20).
2) Help the students combine some of the collected words and phrases into sentences about rain. (Try to write two or more sentences.)
3) Have the students complete all or some of the sentences on their student pages. Encourage the capable students to write sentences of their own.

Praising

- Point out good "wet" words and phrases.
- Comment on rain "ideas" that are familiar experiences to many kids.

Polishing

- Instruct the students to rearrange (and add, if necessary) words to make the sentences interesting.
- Direct the students to give their sentences variety by including questions, exclamations, and statements.

Showing Off

- Hang a large umbrella from the classroom ceiling.
- Have the students cut large raindrops from poster board and write "wet" words, phrases, or sentences on them.
- Glue a clothespin to the back of each raindrop.
- When the glue is dry, clip the raindrops around the edge of the umbrella.

A Slushy, Sloppy Day

The raindrops are _____ and

_____ .

Rain, rain, hurry down to _____

_____ !

Have you ever heard the _____

rain go _____ ,

_____ against your window?

I love to go out on a _____ ,

rainy day and _____

_____ .

Oh, how the rain comes _____ and _____ !

I hear the _____ of _____

water going _____ .

Add one of your own!

Oh, how the rain splashes and splatters, drips and patters!

Fat, wet drops plop on tiny puddles.

The slushy puddle splashes on my legs and leaks into my boots.

After the rain, the air is full of wetness.

Rushing rain, are you hurrying down to turn my backyard into mud?

Rain, rain, rush around and rinse the playground clean.

Clouds drain to give the thirsty earth a drink.

Have you ever heard the soft patter of drizzling rain washing your window?

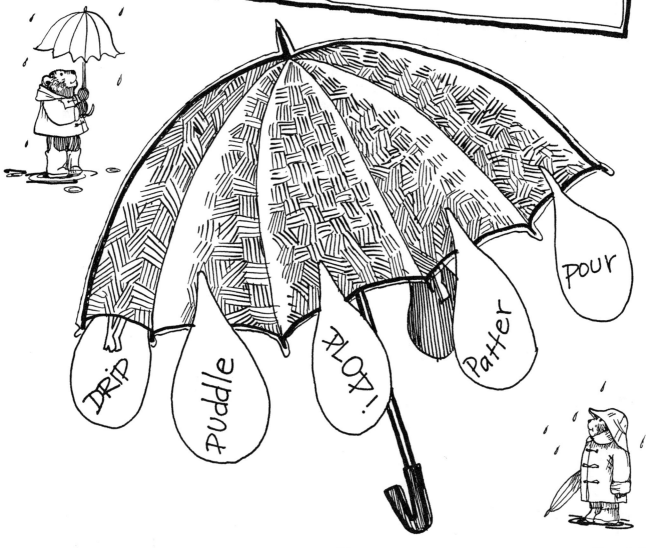

21

4. Paint A Sentence

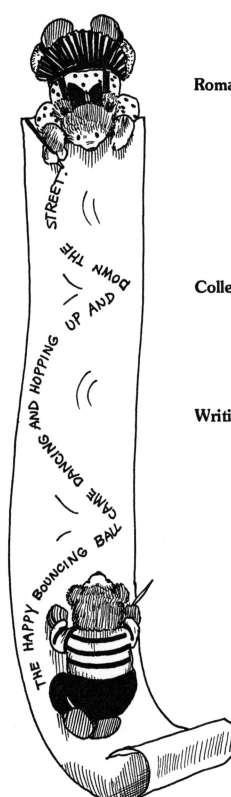

Materials
- large white drawing paper, colored construction paper
- colored chalk, spray fixative
- newspaper
- mural paper

Romancing
- Share the examples of "painted" writing on page 25 with the class. Copy the examples on a large poster or show them on an overhead transparency.
- Discuss how the shape of the writing helps to express what the writing is about. Explain that writing words on paper in a shape to complement what the writing is about is called "painted" writing.
- Have the class brainstorm a list of ideas or topics that would be good for "painted" writings.

Collecting
- Have the class use the student page "A Slithery Snake" (page 24) as a guide to collect ideas for a group "painted" sentence about a snake.
- Write words, phrases, and ideas on the board as the students list them on their papers.

Writing
1) Ask questions to help the students combine words into phrases. For Example:

   What three words describe the snake's appearance?
   What kind of phrase can you write that tells how the snake moves?
   What two or three words sound especially good together?

2) Help the students combine the phrases to build a sentence.

Praising
- Underline or point out good descriptive words--words that describe the movement, sound, or appearance of a snake.
- Look for groups of words that are alliterative or have an interesting rhythm.

Polishing
- Have the students rearrange words or phrases to improve the flow and sound.
- Instruct the students to add at least one good "movement" word (squirm).

Showing Off
- When the group has constructed a polished sentence, have the kids help decide how to write the words on a piece of mural paper in a shape that looks like a moving snake.
- Ask a few students to use a marker to print the words on the mural paper. Several other students may add color around the words with crayon or chalk to visually strengthen the sentence.

MORE PAINTED SENTENCES:
- Repeat the above steps, letting the students choose individual topics.
- Students should first write the words, using a pencil, in large letters on drawing paper to fill much of the space. Only after the words have been written should students add colored chalk. Then the students may go over the words with pens or fine-point markers.
- Spray the chalk drawings with fixative so that the chalk will not smear. Mount the "painted" sentences on colored construction paper.

FRIGHTENING LIGHTNING REACHES DOWN WITH YELLOW FINGERS TO SCRATCH THE GROUND.

A Slithery Snake

How does a snake look?

What sounds does a snake make?

How does the skin of a snake feel?

What kinds of movements does a snake make?

A snake is as sneaky as _____ .

A moving snake reminds me of _____

_____ .

A snake is as slippery as _____

SNAKE SNAKE SNAKE SNAKE SNAKE SNAKE SNAKE SNAKE

THE SNAKE

The scaly, slinky snake slithers slowly, hissing and sneaking across the sands.

THE WAVE

...A WATERY MONSTER, RISING, CLIMBING, SURGING TOWARD THE SKY, NOW FOLDS, ROLLS BACK AND DIGS UNDER ITSELF. IT PLUNGES ON ITS CIRCULAR PATH AND CURLS UNDER ITSELF, LEAVING ONLY A FOAMY REMINDER THAT IT EVER WAS.

Thump, clump, stomp, thump.
Big, loud, giant feet
come clomping and
stomping closer
and closer
to my hiding place.

THE FROG

A wet green frog with bulgy eyes comes leaping and hopping from stone to stone.

25

5. Friends Are Like That

Materials
- a copy of Judith Viorst's ROSIE AND MICHAEL (Atheneum)
- strips of colored construction paper (11 x 1½ inches)
- glue, fine-point markers

Romancing
- Give each student a copy of the student page "Who Needs A Friend?" (page 28).
- Let the students color the two kids on the page.
- Tell the students that each kid on the page needs a friend. Ask the students who would be a good friend for Jennifer, what would the friend be like, and what should the friend do.
- Let the students talk about their friends (what they like about their friends, what their friends do for them, etc.).

Collecting (may be done at the same time as "romancing")
- Help the class make several lists of ideas about friends such as these. (Write the lists on the board.)

    What makes someone a friend?
    Things you do for a friend.
    What does it take to be a good friend?
    What kind of friend would you like to have?

- The students may write a few of their ideas, in word or phrase form, on the student page "Who Needs A Friend?" (page 28).

Writing

1) Use the student page "A Friend Is..." (page 29) as a guide to help the students write sentences about friends.
2) The students may finish all or some of the sentences on the page, or they may start their own sentences. Remind the students to use the ideas on the chalkboard, but encourage them to add others.

Praising

- Look for a variety of sentence structure.
- Point out ideas which are familiar to many other people.

Polishing

- Have the students add or substitute words or phrases to make their sentences clearer and more complete.
- Instruct the students to vary sentence patterns.

Showing Off

- Have each student use a pencil to write at least one of his or her polished sentences in neat, large letters on a strip of construction paper. (Ask the students not to write too close to the ends.)
- Have the students go over their sentences with markers.
- Attach the strips together to make a friendship chain by interlocking the strips and gluing the ends together.
- The students may wish to make individual friendship chains or several group chains to hang in the classroom.

YOU CAN TELL YOUR TROUBLES TO A FRIEND.

A FRIEND LETS YOU RIDE HER NEW BIKE.

Who Needs A Friend?

Jennifer

Scott

Describe a friend for each of these kids.

A Friend Is . . .

A friend is someone who _____ .

Friends don't _____ .

_____ is a friendly thing to do.

My friend and I like to _____ .

I would never _____ to a friend.

I'd like a friend that _____ .

My friend _____ always _____ .

You can trust a friend to _____ .

A friend doesn't tell your secrets.

6. Cut It Out!

Materials
- substantial collection of magazines
- scissors, glue, construction paper
- business-sized envelope for each student
- examples of "found" writing made ahead of time (see pages 32 and 33 for ideas)

Romancing
- Ask the class if they think they could write without pens or pencils. Have the class discuss how scissors, glue and magazines might help them write.
- Show the students examples of "found" writing that you've made or give them copies of the examples on pages 32 and 33. Explain that "found" writing is writing made up of words found in magazines

Collecting
- Give each student a magazine, scissors, an envelope, and a piece of colored construction paper (9 x 11 inches).
- Direct the students to cut out words and phrases from the magazine and put them into their envelopes. They should cut out words in large print only. (Allow 30 minutes or more for this.)

Writing
1) Have the students trade envelopes.
2) Tell the students to use some of the words in their envelopes to write one sentence each. The students can write any kind of complete sentence.
3) Explain to the class that they may cut up words to spell other words. (Demonstrate this if necessary.)
4) Have the students arrange their sentences on construction paper. Make sure they do not glue their sentences to the paper until the sentences have been checked and polished.

Praising
- Look for complete and interesting sentences.
- Point out variety in sentence structure.

Polishing:
- Have the students rearrange words, if necessary, to make their sentences clearer.
- Ask the students to try to add words to their sentences.

Showing Off
- Have the students glue their finished sentences to construction paper.
- Students may use markers or crayons to add proper punctuation to the sentences.
- Display the "found" sentences around the room.

TELEVISION IS Devilishly good,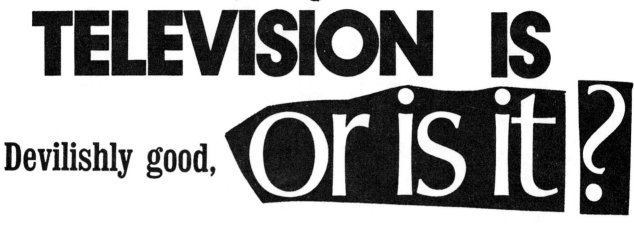

FATHER doesn't Enjoy MY CAKES.

give THE CLOCK to INDIAN THE .

STAY OUT OF THE SOUP.

LIFE is an ADVENTURE.

HIS MOTHER-IN-LAW gives stuffed eggs

TO the FAMILY.

WIN Bath Linens FOR Your CUPBOARD.

WOMEN wear Lacy FASHIONS.

TAKE TIME out for Breakfast.

7. Fancy Footwork

Materials
- collection of old shoes (students may contribute--the shoes needn't be pairs)
- crayons, scissors, markers, and lightweight poster board (white)

Romancing
- Have each student take off one shoe and lay it sideways on a piece of poster board. Then each student should trace around the shoe with a pencil.
- After the students cut out their shoes, direct each student to draw and color the details on his or her shoe.
- Show the class the collection of old shoes. Let the students talk about who the owner of each shoe might have been and where the shoe might have "walked" in its lifetime.

Collecting
- Ask the students to pretend that all of the shoes (including their own) can talk and feel. Discuss what it would be like to be a shoe and what different shoes might say to the people who wear them.
- Help the class make the following lists. Write the lists on the board.
  - things that might happen to shoes
  - places shoes might go
  - different kinds of people (or creatures) who wear shoes
  - complaints that shoes might have

WE JUST LIKE SHOES, I GUESS!

Writing

1) Give each student a copy of the student pages "Whose Shoes?" and "And More Shoes..." (pages 36 and 37).
2) Tell the students to choose four shoes from the old shoe collection to add to their own shoes. (Vary this number according to writing ability.)
3) For each shoe, the students should write a question that the shoe might ask the person who wore it.

Praising

- Look for imaginative questions.
- Point out questions that are written clearly.

Polishing

- Instruct the students to add or rearrange words to make their questions interesting or funny.

Showing Off

- Have each student choose one question to write or glue on the shoe drawing made earlier. (Students can make new shoe drawings to match their questions if time permits.)
- Display the shoes and questions in "footstep" fashion by taping them to the wall.

Whose Shoes?

Example:
Don't you ever
get tired of
romping and
stomping in puddles?

_____
_____
_____

_____
_____
_____

_____
_____
_____

_____
_____
_____

And More Shoes . . .

_____

_____

_____

_____

_____

_____

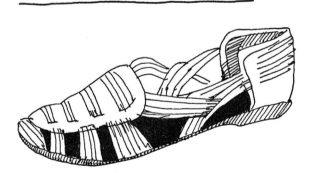

_____

_____

Example:

How would you like to be kicked across the floor every night?

37

8. Extra-Terrestrial Excitement

> DON'T CORNICE ME WITH QUESTIONS WHILE I'M DANCING THE MACABRE!

Materials
- U.F.O.s, made ahead of time (see patterns on page 40)
- poster board
- scissors and markers

Romancing
- Hang several U.F.O.s (with "unidentified" words written on them) from the ceiling or on a bulletin board.
- Discuss the expressions "extra-terrestrial" and "U.F.O."
- Let the students talk about where the U.F.O.s might have come from and what the "unidentified" words on them might mean.

Collecting
- Have the class make up definitions for the unidentified words. Encourage the students to make a variety of definitions by showing them how a word can be a verb, noun, or other part of speech.
- Help the class put the words in several different sentences. Students may write the sentences on the board or they may say them aloud.

Writing
1) Give each student a copy of the student page "U.F.O. Alert" (page 41), and ask the students to "identify" each object by writing what each word might mean on the provided lines.

And/Or

2) Have each student write one sentence with two of the "unidentified" words on a sheet of drawing paper. Let the students draw U.F.O.s around their sentences.

BOYCOTT
—a bed for boys

ABRUPT
—a loud burp—

Praising
- Look for definitions that are clear and understandable.
- Point out imaginative and unusual definitions. Tell the writer why you especially like the definition.

Polishing
- Instruct the students to reread each definition for clarity. If words are still "unidentifiable", writers should add details to their definitions.
- Encourage the students to rearrange their sentences to make them more exciting or outlandish.

Showing Off
- Have each student make a large U.F.O. from poster board (of any design).
- Instruct the students to write an "unidentified" word on each U.F.O. (They may find these in the dictionary or they may make them up.)
- Suspend the finished U.F.O.s from the ceiling for display. Have the class try writing poems using the "unidentified" words.
- Have the students take time to learn the actual meanings of the "unidentified" words.

ARE
YOU
A
CARNIVOROUS
E.T.?

Definitions

Teacher– Use these simple samples as patterns for your own U.F.O.s

U.F.O. Alert!

41

9. Backwards Beasts

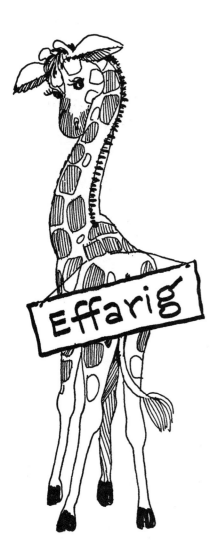

Materials
- crayons, scissors, markers, glue
- construction paper of all colors
- old magazines
- assortment of wallpaper samples (if possible)
- BACKWARDS BEASTS FROM A TO Z, by Albert G. Miller (Bowmar)--optional

Romancing
- Ask the students to bring pictures of animals to class and/or cut out as many animals as they can find in magazines. Ask them to find a number of different animals.
- Have the class talk about how the animals' names would be pronounced *backwards*. (For example, giraffe would be effarig -- EF-a-rig.)
- Ask the students to pretend that each animal's name spelled backwards is the name of a new beast. Have the class share ideas about what those new beasts might look like.
- If possible, read the class BACKWARDS BEASTS FROM A TO Z. Give each student a copy of the student page "Backwards Beasts To Turn Around" (page 45). Read and enjoy the poems together. Let the students figure out the answers and draw the missing beasts.

Collecting
- On the board, collect a list of as many animal names as you can brainstorm together. For each one, print the name forwards and backwards.
- Then collect a list of words and phrases that describe the beasts (appearances, sounds, habits, etc.).
- Hand out the student page "Making Your Own Beast" (page 44). Use the page as a guide to help the students gather ideas for individual descriptions of beasts. Go through the top portion of the page together. Each student can do the bottom alone, or the whole class can do it together.

Writing

1) Have each student try to write a poem describing a beast.
2) The poems may rhyme in an a-a-b-b scheme or an a-b-a-b scheme.
3) Remind the writers that the last word of the poem (the beast's name written frontwards) must be left off.

Praising

- Point out especially colorful, fun, or "beastly" words.
- Look for good uses of rhyme patterns.

Polishing

- Have the students polish their rhymes. Students may help one another find words and phrases that rhyme well. (This might involve choosing a different animal name. Some rhyme more easily than others.)

Showing Off

- Using wallpaper (or magazine pages with patterns and pictures) and other paper, the students may create beasts to match their descriptions.
- Mount the beasts on colored construction paper with the polished poems. Write the animal's original name (the name before it was spelled backwards) on the back of the paper.
- Hang the poems and pictures so that everyone can try to solve the riddles. You might also bind the riddles in book form and circulate the book among the other classes. (Laminating the pages will make them more durable.)

NOIL

Don't try dancing with a Noil
His blood might just begin to boil.
He's mean enough to start you cryin'—
Almost as fierce as a frontwards _____!

EFFARIG

The slimy, squirmy Effarig
Prickly, pink, and pretty big,
Touch it and you'll have to laugh
! Because forward it's a tall _____!

Making Your Own Beast

Animal's name _____frog_____   Name backwards _____gorf_____

Rhyming words:
   hog
   bog
   log
   dog

Descriptive rhyming words:
   hair--fair, there, care, tear
   fangs--gangs
   teach--reach, beseech
   claws--jaws, paws
   tail--stale, jail, fail, sail
   nose--rose, toes, close, hoes
   feet--neat, beat, cheat, heat

NOW YOU DO THE SAME WITH YOUR BEAST!

Animal's name _____   Name backwards _____

Rhyming words: Descriptive rhyming words:

Backwards Beasts To Turn Around

The Tarrop

The *torrap* has such awful teeth,
Three up above and six beneath.
Turn him around and give him a carrot,
He's just a friendly, chatty _____ .

The *Raeb* is a nasty beast,
All black with shaggy hair.
Frontwards he isn't scary
   in the least,
He's just a cuddly _____ .

The Raeb

The Liauq

Long whiskers grow on a *liauq's face*,
And she's got scales all over the place,
Even on her powerful tail.
But turned around she's a chubby _____ .

The claws and wings
   upon a *woc*,
Are hard and scratchy
   as a rock.
It howls and growls and snarls--but how!
Turn it around and find a _____ .

The Woc

The Tar

The grumpy *tar* has eighteen feet,
And only dines on roasted meat,
With two big fangs--imagine that!
But turned around he's a little _____ .

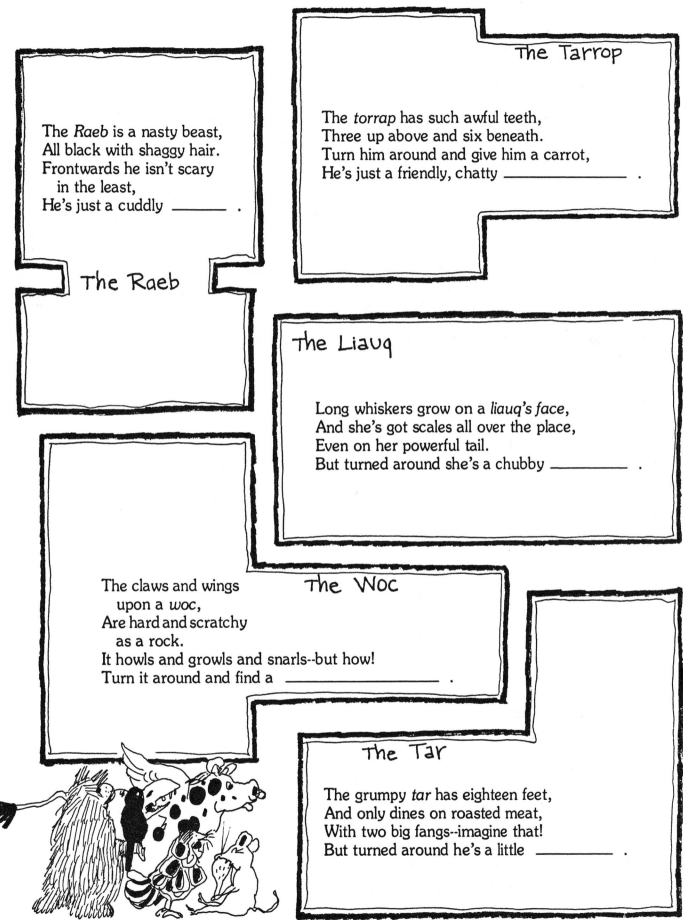

45

10. Words To Chew On

Materials
- 1 apple for each child
- large apple shapes cut from construction paper
- green construction paper, glue, scissors

Romancing and Collecting
- Have the class talk about the look, smell, feel, and color of the apples. Help the class collect words, phrases and ideas that describe the apples. (Label this list 1.)
- Tell the students to bite into their apples. Have the students write words that describe the taste and feel in their mouths. (Label this list 2.)
- Instruct the students to write words that tell how it felt to swallow the apple and how their mouths felt afterwards. (Add these to list 2.)
- Have everyone take another bite of apple. Help the class collect words that describe the sound of the students biting and chewing their apples. (Label this list 3.)
- Help the class collect some similes and comparisons:

Apple, apple, yellow and ripe,
Juicier than the rain.
You taste as sweet as
Kool Aid.
You sound as squeaky
as my wagon
wheels.
You make me think
of a school
lunch.

When everyone in class chews apples it sounds like _____ .
My apple is as sweet as _____ :
This apple tastes like _____ :
I'd rather eat apples than _____ :
_____ reminds me of an apple.
(Label this list 4.)

46

Writing
1) Give each student a copy of the student page "An Apple A Day" (page 48), and instruct him or her to use the page as a guide for writing a poem.
Line 1--choose words from list 1.
Lines 2, 6, and 7--refer to list 4.
Lines 3 and 4--choose from list 2.
Line 5--choose from list 3.
2) Work with the students to guide them in writing each line. (Allow the capable students to add their own ideas or to vary the form.)
3) Have each student create a title for his or her poem.

Praising
- Look for colorful and interesting descriptive words.
- Point out fresh similes.

Polishing
- Have the students try to add several good descriptive words.
- Instruct the students to rearrange words to create a pleasing sound.
- Remind the students to check for correct spelling and mechanics.

Showing Off
- Have the students copy their finished poems onto the paper apple shapes. The students may add construction paper leaves, stems, and an apple worm, just for fun.
- Hang the apples on a class apple tree (made by "planting" a sturdy branch in a pot of gravel).

An Apple A Day

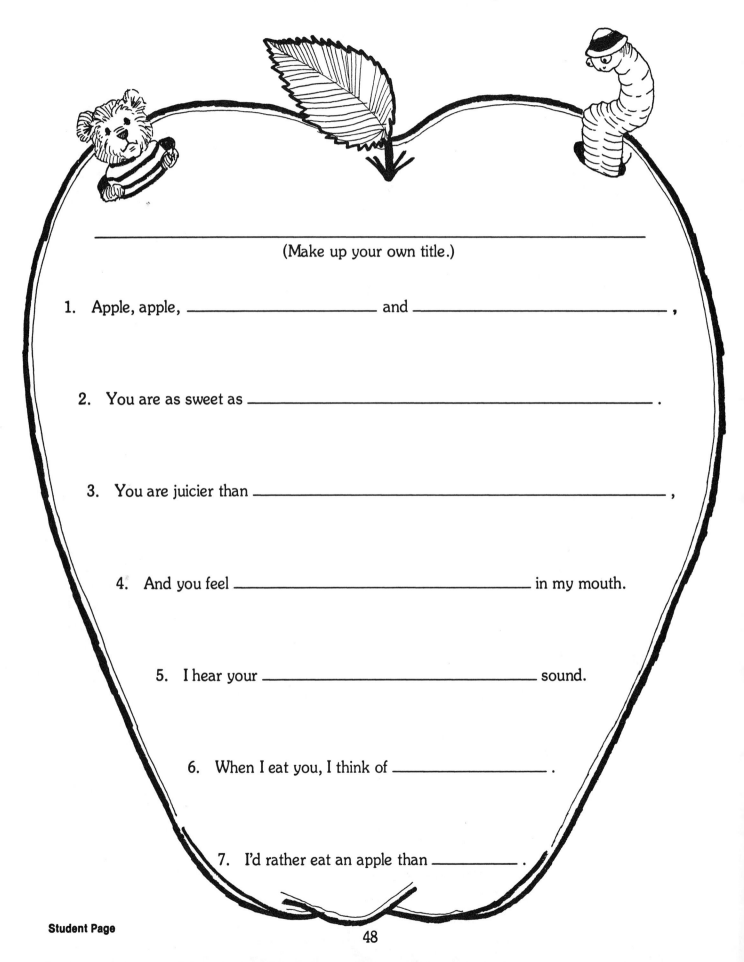

_____
(Make up your own title.)

1. Apple, apple, _____ and _____ ,

2. You are as sweet as _____ .

3. You are juicier than _____ ,

4. And you feel _____ in my mouth.

5. I hear your _____ sound.

6. When I eat you, I think of _____ .

7. I'd rather eat an apple than _____ .

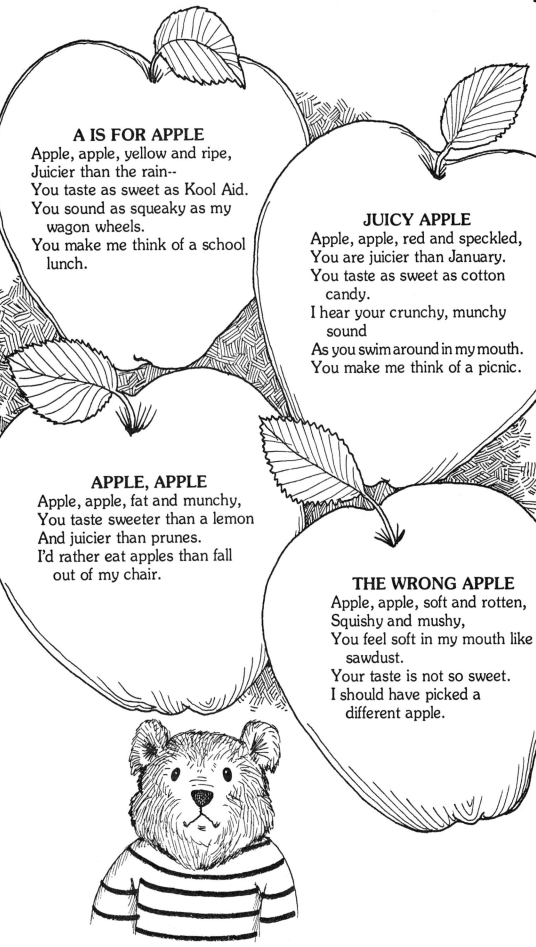

A IS FOR APPLE

Apple, apple, yellow and ripe,
Juicier than the rain--
You taste as sweet as Kool Aid.
You sound as squeaky as my
    wagon wheels.
You make me think of a school
    lunch.

JUICY APPLE

Apple, apple, red and speckled,
You are juicier than January.
You taste as sweet as cotton
    candy.
I hear your crunchy, munchy
    sound
As you swim around in my mouth.
You make me think of a picnic.

APPLE, APPLE

Apple, apple, fat and munchy,
You taste sweeter than a lemon
And juicier than prunes.
I'd rather eat apples than fall
    out of my chair.

THE WRONG APPLE

Apple, apple, soft and rotten,
Squishy and mushy,
You feel soft in my mouth like
    sawdust.
Your taste is not so sweet.
I should have picked a
    different apple.

Example Page

11. Roses, Noses, and Radishes

Materials

- large, white drawing paper
- colored chalk
- spray fixative
- large, colored construction paper
- Mary O'Neill's HAILSTONES AND HALIBUT BONES (if available)

Romancing

- Tell the students a day ahead of time to wear red the next day.
- Read the "red" selection and a few others from HAILSTONES AND HALIBUT BONES (optional).
- Give each student a piece of drawing paper and provide the class with chalk in various shades of red.
- Tell the students to make a design (not a picture) that is mostly red. (They may use one or two other colors, but the design must be predominantly red.)

Collecting

- Ask the following questions to help the class gather lists of "red" ideas, words and phrases.

  List 1 What things *look* red?
  List 2 What things *sound red*?
  List 3 What things *smell red*?
  List 4 How does red *feel*?
  List 5 What makes *you feel* red?
  List 6 What *tastes* red?
  List 7 What *experiences, sights, and ideas* seem red?
  List 8 Can you think of any *places* that look or feel red?

- Encourage the students to "cross senses" in their collecting. For example, red is the winter wind biting my nose (a touch sensation described with a sight word).

Writing

1) Hand out copies of the student page "Red...Red...Red..." (page 52). Help the students form poetry lines, using the student page as a guide.

2) Guiding the students through the student page, one line at a time, tell them to choose words and/or phrases from the collected lists or to add new ones.

Praising

- Point out words that have strong sensory appeal.
- Listen for groups of words that sound good to the ear.
- Comment on interesting titles.

Polishing

- Have the students add any good words or phrases not used.
- Instruct the students to rearrange the lines for a better order, if necessary.
- Direct the students to choose a good beginning line and a good ending line.

Showing Off

- Help the students spray fixative on their chalk designs and then mount the designs on "frames" made of large colored construction paper.
- After the students have copied their polished poems, instruct them to mount the poems on red construction paper and affix the paper to the front or back of their red designs.

More Color Poetry

- Have the students choose another color for which to make other designs and poems. They can follow the same steps and form as above. Hand out more student pages, telling the students to replace the word red with the new color word.
- Display an assortment of the finished products in a "classroom color gallery".

Red ... Red ... Red ... Red ... Red ...

_____ (Title)

Red is _____ and _____ , (list 1)

and the feeling of _____ . (list 4)

Red is the taste of _____ . (list 6)

_____ and _____ smell red. (list 3)

_____ makes me feel red. (list 5)

Red is the sound of _____ and _____ . (list 2)

_____ and _____

_____ are red. (lists 7 & 8)

Red is _____ . (any list)

PICKLES AND STOMACHACHES
Green is lizards and broccoli,
Pickles and the park in spring.
Christmas is green --
So is the croaking of a frog.
Green tastes like spinach and
    moldy cottage cheese.
Loneliness and music are green.
Green is the smell of grass,
And the feeling you have when
    you get sick.

REDDER THAN A ROSE
Sirens screaming,
Stoplights flashing,
Babies crying,
Spaghetti cooking,
These are red.
Red stings your tongue like cinnamon
And bites your nose with cold wind.
Red is angry words
And embarrassment.
Disneyland is red.

BLUE
Going down a waterslide is blue.
Blue is the smell of a pie baking,
And the taste of jam.
My fingers get blue in the winter.
Blue is when your best friend moves away,
Or you get left out of a game.
Blue is oceans and bruises and smoke.
Blue is like sleeping on a soft pillow.

12. 5 To Keep

Materials
- large poster board in various colors
- scissors and crayons

Romancing
- Ask the students to pretend that they've "lost" all of the words in the world except five.
- Have the students think about which five words they would keep.

Collecting
- Give each student a copy of the student page "Just Five" (page 56).
- Ask the students to write the five words on this page, one on each line. (Help them with spelling.) Allow plenty of time for thinking. Share some ideas to help the students.

Writing
1) After each student has chosen five words, ask the students to write one sentence or phrase beside each word to explain why he or she kept that word or why the word is special.
2) Give the students time to share their words with others and to discuss why they kept the words.
3) Have the students reread each word and "explanation" as a line in a poem. Have pairs of students read their poems aloud to one another.
4) Instruct the students to rearrange the order of the lines, if necessary, to make their poems sound better.

Praising

- Look for sentences or phrases which are clear in their explanation of why the word is special.

Polishing

- Have the students rearrange or add words to make each line more understandable.

Showing Off

- Instruct each student to draw and cut out a large numeral five from poster board. (Assist as necessary.)
- Have the students print their completed "five" poems on the numerals.

MY FIVE FAVORITE WORDS ARE "HONEY, NUTTY, GRANOLA, YOGURT, TREATS"!

5 WORDS

Just Five

THE ONLY FIVE WORDS IN THE WORLD
5. 4. 3. 2. 1.

What five words will you keep?

1 _____ _____

_____

2 _____ _____

_____

3 _____ _____

_____

4 _____ _____

_____

5 _____ _____

_____

PURPLE .... my favorite color
BASEBALL .... I don't want to have to stop
playing the game.
FRIENDS .... I need them all the time!
FOOD .... to keep me alive
WISHES .... so I can get other things I need

AMY .... my very best friend
LOVE .... all people need it
HELP .... so I can ask for things
SMILES .... make the world a better place
CHOCOLATE .... I don't want to give it up!

HORSES.....
my favorite
animal

ICE CREAM.....
life is worth living
with ice cream

PARENTS....
for love and
protection

FRIENDSHIP...
everybody
needs
friends

PEACE...
so everyone will
be happy

YES .... to answer questions
NO .... to answer other questions
FOOD .... I need it all the time!
PEOPLE .... Life would be boring without
them.
HOME .... a good place to be

57

13. I've Got Rhythm

Materials
- music selections of interest to students
  (some or all without words)
- tape player or record player
- white drawing paper, colored construction paper
- scissors, pencils, crayons

Romancing
- Play several different musical selections, encouraging the students to move and dance to the music.
- Have the class talk about each selection, discussing what the music makes them think, feel, etc.

Collecting
- Choose one new selection of music that you feel will have great appeal to your students and play it through once.
- Play the piece again as you help the students collect words and phrases for each of the following lists. (Write the lists on the board.)

  List 1   What "feeling" does the music express?
  List 2   What might be happening *during* the music?
  List 3   What does the music make you feel like doing?
  List 4   What do you think about as you listen to the music? (a thunderstorm, Halloween, a jumping frog)

Writing
1) Give each student a copy of the student page "It's Music To My Ears" (page 60) to use in writing a "musical" poem. (Show the students the examples on page 61.)
2) Tell the students to write the word "music" on line 1. Help the students write one line at a time, directing them to refer to the numbered lists on the board for ideas. The students may write other ideas or words that come to mind as they're working.

> *Note:* Writers may deviate from the form, somewhat. (See the examples.)

Praising
- Point out good action words.
- Look for words and phrases that create a certain feeling or mood.

Polishing
- Instruct the students to replace ordinary metaphors with fresh ones (lines 3 and 5).
- Ask the students to replace overused words with active, unusual, or colorful words.

Showing Off
- Let the students take turns reading their polished poems to the musical accompaniment. Have the class match the rhythms of each poem to the rhythms of the music.
- Have the students cut large musical notes from construction paper. The students may glue their finished poems on the notes and then hang them from the ceiling.

It's Music To My Ears!

1. _____

2. _____ , _____ , _____
   (Write three words from list 1.)

3. Sounds like _____

   _____ .
   (Choose an idea from list 2.)

4. Makes me feel like _____

   _____ .
   (Choose one or two words from list 3.)

5. Reminds me of _____

   _____ .
   (Choose something from list 4.)

Music--
Busy, bumpy, scratchy.
Sounds like city traffic and
    playground fights.
It makes me feel like wiggling and
    shaking.
Reminds me of a surprise party.

A Rock Selection

Music--
Soft and silly,
Light and sleepy,
Sounding like early morning.
I feel like floating on the water.
Reminds me of watching birds.

A Quiet Classical Piece

Music--
Crash, squash, smash,
Sounds like someone's being chased.
I feel like hiding under a blanket.
Reminds me of a thunderstorm.

A Loud Classical Piece

Music--
Quick and jazzy,
A bouncy ball.
Sounds like mice running on the
    piano.
Reminds me of being dizzy.

A Jazz Selection

Example Page

14. Never Enough Monsters

Materials
- 5-8 pieces of large mural paper
- crayons, pencils, markers
- books about monsters

Romancing
- Read one or more of your favorite stories about monsters to the class.
- Have the class talk about monsters and their favorite monster tales. Ask the students to describe what monsters look like, how monsters sound, and so on.
- Ask each student to think about how he or she might draw a monster. Let the students share ideas orally.
- Divide the students into groups of four or five. Give each group a piece of mural paper and crayons.
- Tell each group to work together to create a monster. Help the group decide who shall make the head, body, legs, arms, tail, etc.
- When the drawings are complete, ask the groups to name and share their monsters.

Collecting

- Work as a class to make seven lists of phrases, words, and ideas about the monster drawings. Write the ideas on the board.

  > how the monsters look
  > how the monsters move
  > what sounds the monsters make
  > what the monsters do
  > what the monsters like and dislike
  > what the monsters eat
  > how you feel about the monsters

Writing

1) Give each student a copy of the student page "One More Monster" (page 64) to use as a guide for writing a monster poem. Guide the students through the page one line at a time. (They may write about the monsters they've drawn or about any other monster.)

2) When a few lines have been written, help the students organize their lines.
   - Find a good beginning line. Number this line 1.
   - Which line makes a good ending? Put an E by this line.
   - Experiment to find a good order for the lines and number the lines.
   - Make up a good title for the poem.

Praising

- Point out catchy beginnings and interesting endings.
- Look for especially good descriptive words.

Polishing

- Instruct the students to eliminate any lines that are too much alike.
- Have the students shorten any long lines.
- Ask the students to add more detailed lines, if necessary, to describe their monsters.

Showing Off

- Post the large monster drawings around the room.
- Have the students mount their monster poems on colored construction paper and display them in groups around the monster pictures.

One More Monster

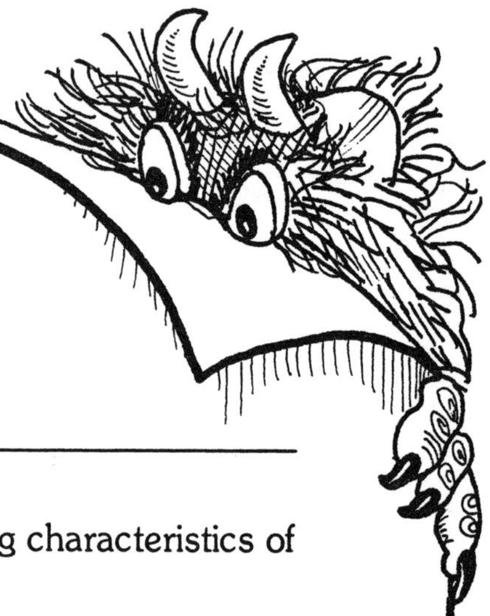

What is your monster's name? _____

Write a line that explains or describes each of the following characteristics of your monster:

what it looks like (eyes, nose, claws, hair, teeth, feet)

_____

_____

what sounds it makes _____

_____

what kinds of things it does _____

_____

what it likes _____

_____

what it doesn't like _____

_____

anything else you want to add _____

_____

THE GOOZLESNORK

Thump, thump, snort, clomp.
Here comes the frightful Goozlesnork.
It swallows trees with a noisy "munch".
It feasts on alligators at night.
It gobbles boys and girls for lunch.
So, keep your door locked very tight
If you don't want a terrible scare.
And never, ever turn out your light --
The Goozlesnork could be anywhere!

THE FRIENDLY MONSTER

Don't be afraid of my Fuzzwuzzwuzz,
He'll never hurt a flea.
His smiley eyes and fluffy fur
Are soft and warm to me.
He may look big
And he sure looks hairy,
His teeth are long
And his horns are scary.
But down inside he's calm and kind
And gentle as a teddy bear.
So come and visit my Fuzzwuzzwuzz.
Hug him all you want--I don't care.

HORRIBLE, HORRIBLE

Monsters come in many sizes,
But there isn't one as gigantic
Or as horrible as the Lapashark.
Three tails each have scratchy scales,
Two heads each have purple eyes,
Six arms each have seven claws,
And the growling it does will chill you cold.
Stay away from the Lapashark,
Never feed it carrots.
They turn it into a howling fiend
And start it breathing fire.

15. Self Silhouettes

Materials
- large, black construction paper
- pencil, scissors
- large construction paper, various colors
- glue

Romancing
- Make a silhouette of each student's profile. You can do this in two ways:
  1) Hang black paper on the wall. Have the student sit sideways in front of the paper, and shine the light from a filmstrip projector on the student's head to cast a shadow on the paper. As the student sits very still, draw around his or her shadow with chalk. Cut out the silhouette.
  2) Have the student lay his or her head sideways on a piece of black paper on a desk or table. Use chalk to draw around the profile, staying about an inch away from the head. Cut out the silhouette.
- The students may glue their silhouettes to a construction paper backing of any color.

Collecting
- Ask the students to think about the following ideas. As they brainstorm, write a list for each idea on the board.

  things I do well
  things I do not do well
  things I like about myself
  things I wish were different about myself
  things I like
  things I don't like
  things I wish for
  things I don't wish for

Writing
1) Give each student a copy of the student page "About Myself" (page 68).
2) Guide the students through the page one line at a time to help them write poems about themselves.
3) The students may change words or rearrange any of the "starters" on the student page (see page 69 for variations).

Praising
- Comment on pairs of lines that sound good together.
- Look for a variety in the kinds of lines written.

Polishing
- Have the students cross out any uninteresting lines.
- Students should cross out any lines that are too much alike.
- Instruct the students to rearrange the lines, if necessary, to make a more interesting order.

Showing Off
- Have the students carefully print their poems on white paper.
- The students may mount their poems on their silhouettes. Display the finished silhouettes around the room.

About Myself

I'm good at _____ .

I'm not so good at _____ .

I'm glad about my _____ .

I'd be glad if _____ .

I like _____ .

I don't like _____ .

I wish _____ .

I don't wish for _____ .

I'm good at skating.
I'm not good on skis.
My hair makes me glad.
My crooked teeth make
  me sad.
I like my friend Jenny.
I don't like bossy people.
I wish for summer,
But I don't wish for
  homework.

My favorite things are
  pizza and stickers,
But I don't like
  spinach at all.
I'm a very good gymnast
But I'm not a good fighter.
I like my family,
But my little
  sister bugs me.

I'm a really good
  climber,
But I'm terrible on a
  skateboard.
I'm glad about my
  thick, warm fur.
I'm not so glad about
  having to sleep all
  winter!

16. Wiggly Squiggly Worms

Materials
- molding clay to make worms (see recipe, page 73)
- real worms, if possible
- construction paper, glue, string, crayons, markers
- 4-inch-wide circle pattern, scissors

Romancing
- Have the class make worms using molding clay, or provide real worms for the class to watch and touch.
- Let the class talk about how worms look, feel and move. Encourage the students to tell stories about "experiences" they've had with worms.

Collecting
- Work with the students to gather the following lists of ideas, words, and phrases about worms. Write the lists on the board.
  - words that describe how worms *look*
  - words that describe how worms *feel*
  - words that describe how worms *smell*
  - words that describe how worms *move*
  - words that describe how worms make *you feel*

Writing
1) Give each student a copy of the student page "Squirmy Worms" (page 72).
2) Help the students use the page as a guide for writing a poem about worms.

3) If needed, give the students suggestions for other lines to add at the end of their poems. For example:
   - worms you don't like
   - why worms are great
   - how to catch a worm
   - the best thing about worms
   - who likes worms best
   - why you don't like worms

Praising
- Look for very descriptive words and phrases.
- Comment on interesting endings.

Polishing
- Have the students replace ordinary words with words that have a strong sensory appeal.
- Ask the students to listen to the lines as they read their poems. Students should rearrange the order of the lines if necessary to make their poems sound better.

Showing Off
- Have each student cut several circles out of colored construction paper and glue them together to form a long worm. The students may add eyes and other "decorations".
- Have the students print their poems on cards and hang the cards around the necks of the worms with string.

Squirmy Worms

I like worms . . .

_____ worms,

_____ worms,

_____ worms,

_____ worms,

_____ worms,

_____ worms,

_____ worms,

_____ worms,

Worms that _____ ,

Worms that _____ ,

Worms that _____ ,

Worms that _____ ,

Worms that _____ ,

And worms that _____ ,

_____

_____

_____

_____

_____

My finished poem is much better than my first one!

MOLDING CLAY RECIPE

2	Cups Salt	2	Cups Boiling Water
1½	Cups Oil	5-10	Drops Food Coloring
2	Tb. Alum	6-8	Cups Flour

- Put the salt, oil, and alum in a large bowl.
- Add boiling water and food coloring.
- Stir in 4 cups of flour with a spoon. Then "knead" in the rest of the flour with your hands until the mixture is of a clay consistency. (You may not need all of the flour.) Be careful not to get the dough too stiff. The dough will thicken as it sits.
- Continue kneading the dough until it is smooth and cool.

I like worms...

Big worms,
Little worms,
~~Fat~~ *fast* worms,
~~Thin~~ *slow* worms,
~~Fast~~ *sassy* worms,
~~Slow~~ *flashy* worms,
Dull worms,
Glow worms —
Worms that giggle
~~Worms that~~ *As they* wiggle,
Worms that curl
And Worms that hump
Worms that scurry,
~~worms that~~ *In a* hurry
Worms that slither
worms that slump.
One kind of worm,
I say with haste,
I ~~don't~~ *Do Not* ~~much~~ like
Is a worm with taste!

I like worms...

Big worms,
Little worms,
Fast worms,
Slow worms,
Sassy worms,
Flashy worms,
Dull worms
Glow worms —
Worms that giggle
As they wiggle,
Worms that curl
And worms that hump,
Worms that scurry
In a hurry,
Worms that slither
Worms that slump
But
One kind of worm,
I say with haste,
I Do Not like
Is a worm with taste!
by Shana M. Grade 3

Example Page

73

17. Riddles In The Air

Materials

- blown-up balloons, each tied to string
- writing paper and pencils
- colored construction paper
- permanent markers, scissors

Romancing

- Have the students stand up, holding their balloons, and spread out across the room. Decide on a signal for getting quiet to listen. Then, give directions such as the following:
    - Punch your balloon away from you as you hold onto the string. See how many times you can do this.
    - Rub your balloon against your hair and then stick it to your clothes.
    - Play catch with a partner, tossing balloons back and forth.
    - Hit your balloon high into the air. Try to keep the balloon in the air with 10 hits.
    - Hit your balloon high into the air. Try to keep the balloon in the air by bouncing it off your head 10 times.

Collecting

- Have the students sit down and tie their balloons to their wrists or to their chairs.
- Help the students make a list on the board of words that describe the way the balloons look or feel. Label this list 1. (red, bouncy, rubbery, light, smooth)
- Have the kids lightly pinch and rub their balloons, listening to the different sounds.
- Have the class make a list of sound similes for the balloons by having them think of several ways to complete this phrase:

    sounds like _____

    (sounds like a screeching whistle)

    Label this list 2.
- Have the class make a list of words that end in "ing" which describe the movement or action of the balloons. Label this list 3. (floating, fleeing, bouncing, escaping, flying)
- Have the class make a list of phrases that describe places or situations where you might find balloons. Label this list 4. (parade, circus, surprise party, Disneyland)

Writing

- Give each student a copy of the student page "Who Am I?" (page 76). Have the students follow the format below for writing riddles. The teacher should direct the writing for each line, drawing attention to the lists collected on the board.

Line 1	Fill in the blanks with three words from list 1.
Line 2	Fill in the blanks with one simile from list 2.
Line 3	Choose three words from list 3.
Line 4	Choose four places from list 4.
Line 5	Write "Who Am I?"
Title	Add a title that *does not* give away the answer to the riddle.

Praising

- Point out interesting and unusual descriptive words.
- Look for interesting and unusual "ing" words.
- Notice good combinations of words.

  (Bobby, I like the way you wrote "bobbing, bouncing, bursting"!)

Polishing

- Have the students look carefully at each line by asking themselves the following questions:

  Do I like the words I've chosen? If not, can I replace them with better words?

  Do I like the order of words in each line? If not, can I change the order of the words to make the line better?

Showing Off

- Have the students write their finished poems on clean paper and then mount them on small pieces of construction paper. They may punch holes in the poems and attach them to the strings of the balloons.

OR

Instruct the students to cut balloon shapes from colored construction paper, write their poems on the shapes and hang the balloon shapes from the ceiling.

OR

Suggest that the students write their poems directly onto their balloons with a permanent marker.

Who Am I?

Write a riddle with the help of ideas from the board or your own new ideas.

_____ (Title)

I am _____ , _____ , and _____ .

I sound like _____

_____ .

Watch me _____ , _____ ,

and _____ .

You'll find me at _____ and _____ ,

at _____ and _____ .

_____ .

CAN YOU GUESS?

I am shiny, slippery, and purple.
I sound like a whooshing wind.
Watch me go diving, dropping,
and drooping. You'll find me
at parades and parties, at
celebrations and circuses.
Who am I?

GUESS WHO?

I'm red and rubbery.
I sound like a squealing piglet.
Watch me rising, bouncing, and
escaping. You'll see me at
grand openings, amusement parks,
and at a birthday party!
Who am I?

DO YOU KNOW WHO?

Blue and bouncy and bold--that's me.
If you rub me I sound like chalk
screeching across the chalkboard.
Watch me soaring, sailing, and
surprising--but I hope not popping.
Look for me at the county fair or
in a clown's hand. Can you guess
who I am?

Note:
Some riddles will deviate
from the exact format
shown in the lesson--this is
fine. Encourage creativity!

18. Lots Of Lists

Materials
- large numbers (1-10) written on chalkboard
- hangers, masking tape
- long strips of paper (about 24 inches each)

Romancing
- Ask the students what the first thing they do in the morning is and what other things they do soon after waking up.
- Give everyone a chance to talk about his or her morning routines.
- Have the class make a list of "the first 10 things you should do in the morning". Write the list on the board.

Collecting
- Give each student a copy of the student page "That Makes Me Mad!" (page 80).
- Let the students take turns discussing things that make them mad. Write a list on the board.
- Give the students time to make their own lists on the student page, using the ideas from the board and/or others that apply to them personally. (They should collect more than 10.)

Writing
1) Have the students work in pairs to review their lists. Instruct each pair to do the following.

   - Cross out any ideas that are like others.
   - Cross out any ideas that are not interesting.
   - Choose the 10 best ideas.

2) Have each pair read over their lists together to make sure each item is clear and easy to understand.

Praising
- Look for interesting or surprising items on the lists.
- Comment on examples with which other people can easily identify.

Polishing

- Have the students find the best order for the lines. They should think about which lines will make good beginnings or endings.
- Have the students try to add an active word to each line, or a word that expresses a "mad" feeling.

Showing Off

- Instruct the students to write their polished lists on long strips of paper, being sure to include the titles. Students may want to add a "mad" drawing, too. (Tell them not to write on the top two inches of paper.)
- Help the students attach the paper strips to hangers by folding the top two inches over the hanger and taping the paper on the back.
- Display the lists by hanging them with a wire from the ceiling, hallway, or window, etc.

Other Lists

- After the students have finished these lists, they may try making other kinds of lists.

Things To Do Before Bed	Things To Beware Of
Questions Never To Ask	Things To Do For A Friend
Things That Should Be Changed	Things Never To Do
Things To Say "No" To	Things Not To Do In School

That Makes Me Mad!

Make a list of some things that make you mad.

_____

_____

_____

_____

_____

_____

_____

_____

_____

_____

_____

_____

Draw a picture of yourself in the box looking mad!

Things That Make Me Mad...
1. Grouchy people
2. When I trip on my shoelaces
3. When I get blamed for something my brother did
4. Not being able to find my jeans
5. Falling off my skateboard in front of people
6. When people tease me
7. People who get in line in front of me
8. Being the littlest kid in the family
9. Losing my pencil
10. When I can't spell a word I want to write

Things To Do In The Morning
1. Wake up
2. Yawn
3. Poke my brother
4. Brush my teeth
5. Take off my P.J.'s
6. Get dressed
7. Eat breakfast
8. Make my lunch
9. Kiss my mother
10. Leave for school

THINGS THAT SHOULD BE CHANGED

1. THE LENGTH OF SUMMER
2. THE NUMBER OF WARS
3. T.V. CHANNELS
4. DOLLAR BILLS
5. THE RULE ABOUT NOT EATING SO MUCH SUGAR
6. THE COST OF TOYS
7. DIRTY SOCKS
8. BURNED-OUT LIGHT BULBS
9. LENGTH OF RECESS
10. DIAPERS

Example Page

19. Goldfish Gossip

Materials

- bowl or tank with goldfish
- white drawing paper
- crayons
- large paintbrush
- scissors
- blue tempera paint
- water
- plain paper
- newspaper

Romancing

- Bring a bowl or tank of live goldfish to class.
- Have the class stand around the tank and watch the fish eat and swim. Encourage the students to talk about what they see.
- Ask the students to imagine what the fish might be thinking and what they might be saying to each other.

Collecting

- Let the class talk more about the kinds of things fish might say to each other.
- Have the class make a list of topics that fish might discuss. Write the list on the board.
- Have the class make a second list of words that fish might use. (Encourage them to think of "watery" or "fishy" words.)
- Help the class brainstorm some possible conversations that fish might have.

Writing

1) Instruct the class to write a few brief fish conversations.
   Help the students begin by writing on the board or saying aloud the start of a dialogue.
   (Does this kid really think we like this grainy food he gives us every day?)
   Let the students decide what the reply might be.
2) Give each student a copy of the student page "Goldfish Gossip" (page 84).
3) Have the students write a conversation for one or more of the pairs of fish on the page. For each fish, the students should write one complete statement or question.

Praising
- Let the students share their conversations with one another. Compliment the writers on funny, unusual, or interesting words.
- Notice conversations that have a surprising or amusing twist.

Polishing
- Have the students make sure that both statements make sense.
- Instruct the students to replace ordinary words or phrases with more interesting words or phrases.
- The students should make sure that both parts of their conversations are complete sentences with proper punctuation and capitalization.

Showing Off
Have the students make fishbowl resists to display their poems.

1) On white drawing paper, have the students draw and color a fishbowl scene which includes fish, underwater plants, and whatever else they want to include. (It is crucial that the items be colored heavily with crayons, excluding the color blue.)
2) Mix a thin wash of blue tempera paint. Assisting one student at a time, help the students paint a light coat of blue tempera wash over their papers. The paint will not stick to the crayon if the crayon is applied heavily and if the paint is applied quickly and thinly.
3) Have each student cut out the "talk balloons" from one goldfish conversation on the student page.
4) When the paint is dry, the students may glue their "talk balloons" near two of the fish on their pictures.
5) Instruct the students to trim the edges of their pictures in a rounded fashion to give them a fishbowl shape.

Goldfish Gossip

85

20. Hats Off To You!

SALE
Buy this comfortable, floppy hat for just $4.00.
✓ Keep Dry In The Rain.
✓ Keep Warm In The Wind.
✓ You'll Love The Flower.

Materials
- assorted hats (students may contribute)
- crayons, markers, scissors, glue
- stiff poster board or cardboard
- mirror
- Berenstains' OLD HAT, NEW HAT (Random House)

Romancing
- Gather several hats of as many different styles as you can find.
- Display the hats in the classroom. Let the students take turns trying on the hats. (Have the mirror handy!) The students may talk about how they look in the hats, who might have worn the hats, etc.
- Read OLD HAT, NEW HAT to the class.
- Give each student a copy of the student pages "Hats, Hats, and More Hats" (pages 88 and 89).
- Let the students color the hats on page 88. Then the students may cut out the hats and glue them to each of the heads on page 89.

Collecting
- Have the class gather the following lists. (Write the lists on the board.)
  - words that describe hats (colors, shapes, textures, appearances, sizes, decorations, etc.)
  - uses for hats (other than the obvious one!)
  - things that are special about a certain hat

Writing

1) Tell the students that they each should choose a hat from the classroom collection or from the student page.

2) Help the students write short ads for the hats they've chosen, using the ideas and words collected. The ads should try to answer the following questions. (Write the questions on the board.)

- How does the hat look or feel?
- What's special about the hat?
- Who should buy the hat?
- Where would someone wear the hat?
- What other uses does the hat have?

Note: To help the writers get started, have the entire class do a sample ad on the board.

Praising

- Look for colorful words or phrases that describe the hats.
- Point out phrases that would convince someone to buy the hat.

Polishing

- Have the students shorten long ads by eliminating unnecessary ideas or words.
- Ask the students to add at least one word or phrase to make their ads more convincing.

Showing Off

- Direct the students to rewrite and illustrate their polished ads on poster board. Display the ads with the hats on a display table.

Hats, Hats, and More Hats

89

21. Mud, Marvelous Mud

Materials
- mud or dirt
- water
- sticks, pebbles, stones, moss, etc.
- plastic containers, tinfoil pie plates

Romancing
- Let the students spend a half-hour or so, indoors or outdoors, making mud pies. Have the students work in groups of two or three.
- As the students are working, suggest that they think carefully about what they will put into and on top of the pies. Tell the students to pay attention to how they make the pies so that they will be able to tell someone else how to make a mud pie.

Collecting
- As the students are making pies, ask them to think of words or phrases that describe the mud.
- Keep a list of their ideas on large pieces of poster board.
  - smell words, feel words, sound words,
  - phrases describing what mud does and how it moves
  - phrases describing what you can do or make with mud
  - similes beginning: Mud is as gooey as _____ , or mud feels like _____ .

Writing
1) After the mess is cleaned up, give each student a copy of the student page "My Marvelous Mud Pie Recipe" (page 92). Display the collected lists where all of the students can see them.
2) Guide the students in writing their recipes by giving them the following directions. Encourage them to use words and phrases they've collected.
   - Write the ingredients needed for your mud pie recipe.
   - Write the steps for making the pie, in the correct order.
   - Explain how to "cook" the pie.
   - Tell how many people the pie will serve.
   - Think of a delicious name for your recipe.

Praising
- Point out good "muddy" words.
- Comment on clear directions.

Polishing
- Remind the students to make sure that all the parts of the recipe are there: recipe title, ingredients, steps, baking instructions, descriptions of final product.
- Ask the students to add more concrete, colorful "mud" words if they can.

Showing Off
- Have the students paste their rewritten recipes on cardboard and then trim the cardboard like recipe cards. Make a class recipe box to hold the cards. Be sure to plan another pie-making day when the students can try one another's recipes.

OR

Have the students copy their recipes on stiff paper. Instruct them to glue or staple their recipes to sticks that can be "implanted" into the pies. Display the recipes with the pies at a "bake off".

OR

Have a mud pie tea party! The students may bring their favorite stuffed animals to "taste test" the recipes. Arrange the animals artistically in groups as if they were actually having a tea party. Invite parents, the principal, or other classes to view the tea party!

Note: Students may write recipes for other dishes such as cakes, muffins, quiches, casseroles, etc.

My Marvelous Mud Pie Recipe

_____ Serves _____
(name of recipe)

Ingredients: _____

_____

_____

_____

_____

Directions: 1. _____

_____

2 _____

_____

3. _____

_____

4. _____

_____

5. _____

_____

Bake: _____

ALL THIS MUD NEEDS IS A LITTLE HONEY

Mashed Mud Soufflé

(serves 4 people or 400 ants)

1 gallon dirt
2 cups water
3 handfuls grass

1 cup sand
1 cup dandelion fluff
lots of pretty pebbles

1. Add a few drops of water to the sand and then pat the sand into the bottom of a pie pan.
2. Whip the dandelion fluff for 10 minutes.
3. Add the dirt to the dandelion fluff and stir carefully.
4. Pour the water into the dandelion/dirt mixture and "mash" the mixture with your hands.
5. Pat the mud mixture on top of the sand layer.
6. Sprinkle grass on the top and add pebbles for decoration.

Bake the pie in the sun for two days.

Oozing Goozing Nachos

Michael's Whipped Mud Delight

Mud Plop Drop Biscuits

22. Secret Messages

Materials
- supplies for invisible writing (see page 95)
- envelopes

Romancing
- Give each student a copy of the student page "Mystery Letter" (page 96).
- Explain that the letter on the student page is written in code. Show the students how to "translate" the code, and help them with the first few words.
- Give the students time to decipher the letter.

Collecting
- Review the parts of a letter with the class.
- Have the class make a list of good secretive words to be used in "private" letters.
- Help the class collect a list of good topics or ideas for secret letters.

Writing
1) Give each student a copy of the student page "Top Secret" (page 97).
2) Make sure the students clearly understand where the return address, greeting, body, closing, and signature belong.
3) Give the students time to write secret letters. Remind them to use the ideas collected on the board.

Praising
- Look for clear, understandable sentences.

Polishing
- Help the students check their letters to make sure they have followed the proper form.
- Have the students add details to unclear sentences.

Showing Off

- Give the directions below to the students to help them write invisible secret letters!
- Put each invisible letter in an envelope. The students may "mail" or trade envelopes and then follow the directions to make the writing visible again!

HOW TO WRITE INVISIBLY

Gather: paper (without a hard surface)
small brush or cotton swabs
small paper cups of lemon juice

Use a small paintbrush or cotton swab dipped in lemon juice to write your letter. Let the letter dry completely. The writing will be invisible!

HOW TO READ INVISIBLE WRITING

In order for the invisible writing to appear, you must hold the paper close to a source of heat such as a light bulb.

This can be done at school or at home. Carefully hold the paper in front of a light bulb. Pass the paper back and forth over the heat source until the words appear.

Note: The invisible writing will turn brown.

Mystery Letter

41 Givv Ilzw
Yvzigldm, Kz.
Nzb 8, 0234

Wvzi Kfmpb,

Nvvg nv yb gsv srev
zugvi hxsllo. Dv'oo tvg
slmvb.

Blfi uirvmw,
Ufmpb Yvzi

NEVER FEAR,
SHERLOCK
BEAR
IS
HERE

1 2 3 4 5 6 7 8 9 0
↓ ↓ ↓ ↓ ↓ ↓ ↓ ↓ ↓ ↓
0 9 8 7 6 5 4 3 2 1

A B C D E F G H I J K L M
↓ ↓ ↓ ↓ ↓ ↓ ↓ ↓ ↓ ↓ ↓ ↓ ↓
Z Y X W V U T S R Q P O N

N O P Q R S T U V W X Y Z
↓ ↓ ↓ ↓ ↓ ↓ ↓ ↓ ↓ ↓ ↓ ↓ ↓
M L K J I H G F E D C B A

Top Secret!

_____ Address

_____

_____ , _____ Date

Dear _____ , Greeting

_____

_____ Body Of Letter

_____

_____

_____

_____

_____

_____ , Closing

_____ Signature

97

23. We All Scream For Ice Cream

Materials
- supplies for making ice cream (see recipe, page 101)
- supplies for eating ice cream
- colored construction paper, scissors, markers, glue
- circle pattern for making paper ice cream "scoops"
- copy of WHERE THE SIDEWALK ENDS, by Shel Silverstein (Harper Row)

Romancing
- Let the students help make ice cream, according to the directions on page 101, as a class project.
- While they're making the ice cream, let them talk about favorite kinds of ice cream and some of the other ideas listed below in the "collecting" step.
- Read the poem "Eighteen Flavors" from Silverstein's book.

Collecting
- Give each student a copy of the student page "Ice Cream Ideas" (page 100) to use as a guide for gathering ideas, words, and phrases for descriptive paragraphs about ice cream cones.
- As the class brainstorms ideas, write a list of the ideas on the board.

Descriptions

UH-OH

Writing

1) Tell the students to each choose a favorite flavor of ice cream to describe.
2) Work with the students to write a few sample sentences that describe ice cream.
3) Have the students write other sentences which combine some of the collected ideas.
4) Direct the students in combining four sentences to make a descriptive paragraph for each of their ice cream cones.
5) Remind the students to write titles on their descriptions.

Praising

- Look for good descriptive words--words that really help you taste, see, and feel ice cream.
- Comment on interesting titles.

Polishing

- Have the students make sure they have included action words--words that tell what the ice cream does. Ask the students to add at least one more action word.
- Instruct the students to rearrange the order of the sentences, if necessary, to make their descriptions more clear or interesting.

Showing Off

- Help the students cut out circles for scoops of ice cream and triangles for ice cream cones.
- Have the students write words or phrases used in their descriptions on the circles. Instruct the students to write the ice cream flavors on the cones.
- Have the students glue the scoops to the cones. Display the ice cream cones and the finished descriptions on a bulletin board.

Caramel Crunch

Sticks in my teeth
Gooey swirls
Dropping, dripping
Nutty and munchy
Icy cold as winter
Plops on the floor.

Ice Cream Ideas

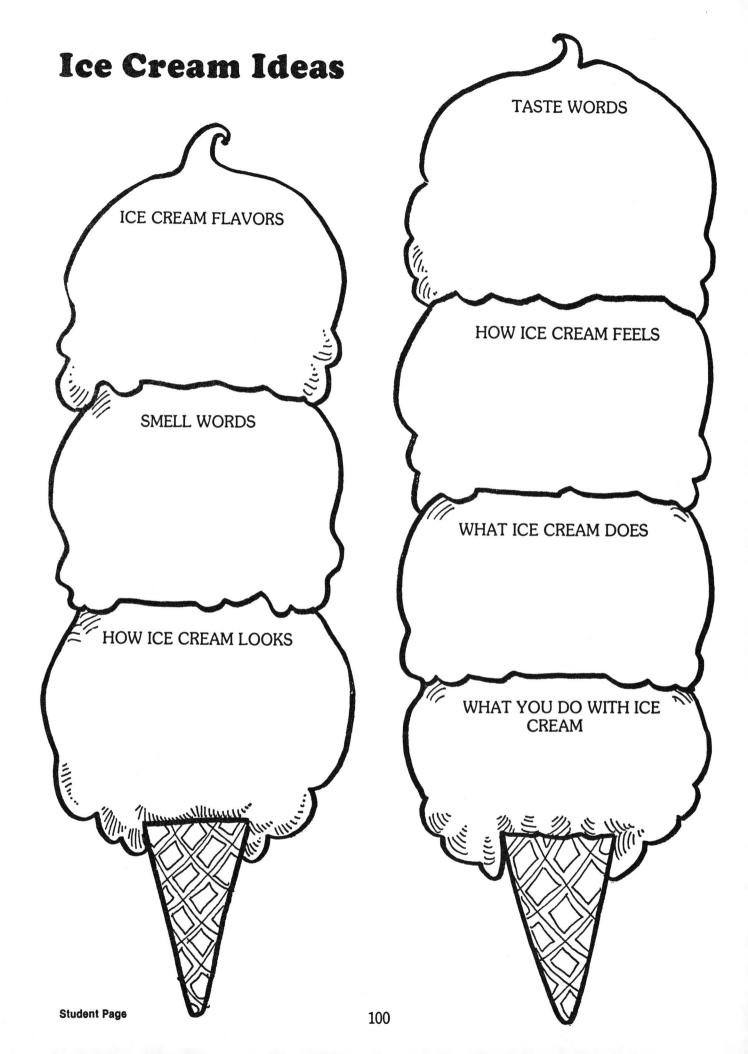

ICE CREAM FLAVORS

SMELL WORDS

HOW ICE CREAM LOOKS

TASTE WORDS

HOW ICE CREAM FEELS

WHAT ICE CREAM DOES

WHAT YOU DO WITH ICE CREAM

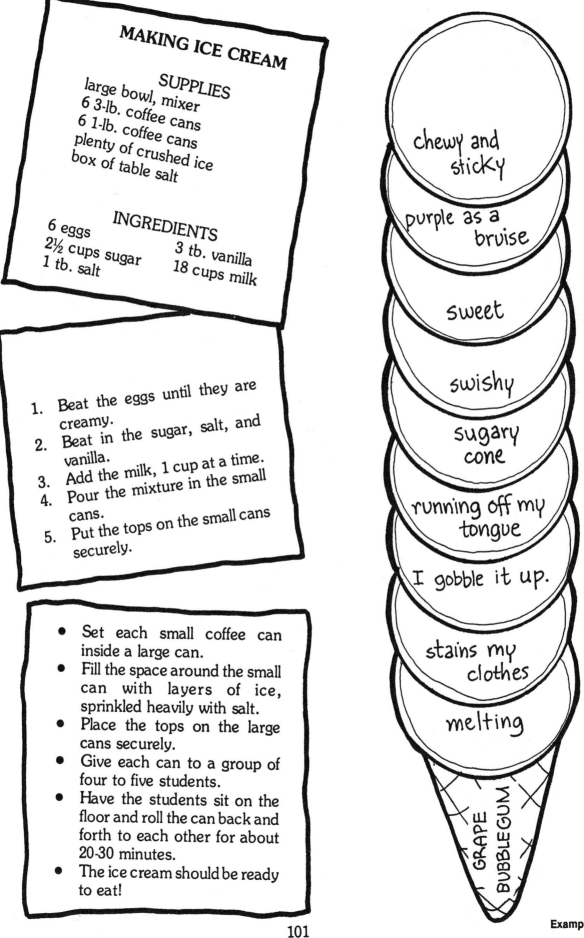

MAKING ICE CREAM

SUPPLIES
large bowl, mixer
6 3-lb. coffee cans
6 1-lb. coffee cans
plenty of crushed ice
box of table salt

INGREDIENTS
6 eggs
2½ cups sugar
1 tb. salt
3 tb. vanilla
18 cups milk

1. Beat the eggs until they are creamy.
2. Beat in the sugar, salt, and vanilla.
3. Add the milk, 1 cup at a time.
4. Pour the mixture in the small cans.
5. Put the tops on the small cans securely.

- Set each small coffee can inside a large can.
- Fill the space around the small can with layers of ice, sprinkled heavily with salt.
- Place the tops on the large cans securely.
- Give each can to a group of four to five students.
- Have the students sit on the floor and roll the can back and forth to each other for about 20-30 minutes.
- The ice cream should be ready to eat!

chewy and sticky

purple as a bruise

sweet

swishy

sugary cone

running off my tongue

I gobble it up.

stains my clothes

melting

GRAPE BUBBLEGUM

Example Page

24. A Character With A-"Peel"

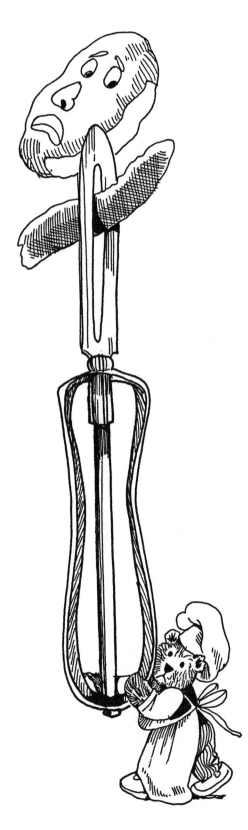

Materials
- large, clean, raw potato for each student
- toothpicks and/or straight pins
- scraps of paper, cloth, yarn, sequins, beads, raisins, marshmallows

Romancing
- Give each student a potato. Tell the students that they are to make a "character" out of the potato.
- Provide odds and ends such as those listed above for the students to use in decorating their potatoes.
- Have the students name their potato characters.

Collecting
- Give each student a copy of the student page "Quite A Character!" (page 104) to guide them in the gathering of ideas and words for writing character descriptions.
- Write a variety of suggestions and ideas on the board so that the writers can choose those appropriate for their own potato characters.

Writing
1) Have the students write descriptive sentences on copies of the student page "Who's This?" (page 105).
2) Encourage the students to add sentences of their own to those suggested on the sheet.
3) Remind the students to make use of the lists collected on their "Quite A Character!" sheets.
4) Have the class discuss ideas for titles. Each student should write a title for his or her description.

Praising
- Point out words and phrases that describe a character well.
- Look for interesting metaphors used to describe characters.

Polishing
- Ask the students to add a few strong, colorful words to their descriptions to make them more interesting.
- Students should rearrange sentences, when necessary, to give their paragraphs good beginnings and endings, or to make their descriptions clear.

Showing Off
- Have the students rewrite their descriptions and glue them onto cards or construction paper.
- Display the descriptions with the "a-peeling" characters, or display the descriptions and characters separately and let visitors try to match them.

Quite A Character!

Potato
character's name _____

Words that tell how he or she looks:

nose	_____
eyes	_____
face	_____
ears	_____
glasses	_____
body	_____
feet	_____
chin	_____
beard	_____

What things the character does:

What kind of person she or he is:

How I feel about this character:

Special things about this character:

Who's This?

_____ is a _____ .
(name)

fellow
lady
man
girl

She (he) has a _____

and a _____ .

He (she) is as silly (strange, funny, bold) as _____

_____ .

She (he) reminds me of _____ .

_____ walks like _____ .
(name)

He (she) likes to _____ .

The strangest thing she (he) does is _____ .

One time _____ _____ .
(name)

Would you believe that he (she) can _____ !

25. Call The Doctor!

MOAN GROAN ⊚ ? ! ⊚

Materials
- the poem "Sick", from Shel Silverstein's WHERE THE SIDEWALK ENDS (Harper Row)
- copy of the book MOTHER, MOTHER, I FEEL SICK, by Remy Charlip (Parents' Magazine Press), if available
- crayons and markers
- construction paper and glue

Romancing
- Read the poem "Sick", and the book by Charlip (listed above), if possible.
- Let the students take turns talking about times they pretended to be sick but really were not. (You take a turn, too!)

Collecting
- Give each student a copy of the student page "Major Ailments" (page 108). (Explain what the words "major" and "ailment" mean.)
- Have the students use page 108 as a guide for gathering ideas that can be used in a "sick" argument.
- Write ideas on the board as the students collect them on their student pages.

Writing

1) Have the students begin writing poems about "faking" illnesses on their copies of the student page "I'm Really, Really Sick!" (page 109).

2) Tell the students to remember that they are writing arguments to convince someone that they really are sick.

3) The ideas at the bottom of the student page can give the students some starters for poetry lines. The students may add others.

Praising

- Look for convincing lines.
- Point out good descriptions of feeling sick.

Polishing

- Have the students make sure they have included descriptive "sick" words in every line.
- Instruct the students to arrange the lines in the order that sounds best, eliminating any lines that are not interesting.
- Students should add good titles to their poems.

Showing Off

- Allow time for the students to draw pictures of themselves being sick (on page 109).
- Direct the students to cut out their pictures, "frame" them with construction paper, and mount the finished poems with their drawings.

Major Ailments

Make a list of sicknesses or health problems.

measles
infected ear
sprained toe

List parts of the body that might hurt.

fingers
head
kneecaps

List words or phrases that describe how *awful* you feel.

horrible
turning green
about to split

List some words that are very convincing.

immediately
truly
honest
deathly ill

SAY AHHH...

I'm Really, Really Sick!

Mother, mother, I can't go to school today.

My _____ feels _____ .

It's so _____ .

My tongue is _____ .

I feel like _____ .

If I get up, I'll _____ .

Besides that, _____ .

My _____ hurts worse than _____ .

I think I'm going to _____ .

DRAW A PICTURE OF YOURSELF LOOKING REALLY, REALLY SICK!

109

26. Poppin' Paragraphs

Materials
- popcorn popper and popcorn ingredients
- 11 x 18 inch (or similar size) pieces of dark poster board
- glue, crayons, markers
- paper towels, paper plates

Romancing
- Let the class make popcorn! (Make enough to eat and an extra batch that is unsalted and unbuttered.)
- As the class enjoys eating the popcorn, encourage them to talk about why the popcorn is good and what they like about it, etc.

Collecting (Do this while you're eating the popcorn.)
- Give each student a copy of the student page "Fresh From The Popper" (page 112) to use as a guide for collecting ideas, words, and phrases about popcorn.
- As the students brainstorm ideas and write them on their papers, keep a list of ideas on the board.

110

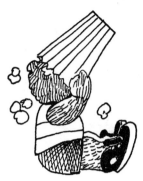

Writing
Direct the writing as follows, one step at a time.

1) Choose some ideas from the collected lists that will help explain why everyone should eat popcorn.
2) Write down phrases or sentences that you could use in convincing people to eat popcorn.
3) Make each phrase into a complete sentence or combine two or more phrases to make a sentence.
4) Cross out any sentences that are too much like others.
5) Choose a good beginning sentence. Number all of the sentences in an interesting order, saving a good sentence for the ending.
6) Think of a good title.

Praising
- Point out words and phrases that describe the sounds, smells, and tastes of popcorn.
- Look for sentences that make a strong argument for eating popcorn.

Polishing
- Have the students add and rearrange words to include some alliterative phrases
- Instruct the students to rearrange sentences, if necessary, to make their paragraphs more interesting or more understandable.

Showing Off
- Help the students mount their finished paragraphs at the bottom of pieces of poster board.
- Let the students use the blank space on the poster board for popcorn art. Students can glue pieces of popcorn on the poster board to make pictures or designs. They may add color on or around the popcorn with markers and/or crayons.

Fresh From  The Popper

Write words that describe popcorn.

The smell: The taste:

The sound: The feel in your mouth:

Why should people eat popcorn? Write your own ideas.

POP, POP, POP

Everybody needs popcorn. It's the only snack that you can watch explode in front of your eyes! The buttery smell and salty taste are so inviting. Just listen to it pop and crunch. How can anyone resist popcorn? It tastes better than ice cream!

THE BEST THING ABOUT POPCORN

The best thing about popcorn is its warm, fresh smell -- or perhaps it is the happy, noisy sound in the pan. No, I think the best thing about popcorn is the buttery flavor of the fluffy white puffs. Yet, even better than the buttery flavor is the bowl that my hand is reaching into right now!

WHAT'S SO GOOD ABOUT POPCORN?

Pop, crackle, hiss. The popcorn is cooking. You can smell it next door. Nothing sounds as crunchy as popcorn, and nothing tastes as fresh and salty. It's good today and it's good tomorrow. Popcorn is not junk food because it's good for you. Have some right now!

113

27. Creepy Crawly Tales

Materials
- large spider web (made by spinning black yarn on a bulletin board)
- black construction paper or poster board
- 4 x 2 inch strips of yellow paper
- yellow, white, orange, green construction paper scraps
- glue, straight pins, scissors

Romancing
- Let the class tell personal tales about spiders they've seen or spider stories they've heard.
- Tell the students that you'd like them to make spiders to live in the web on the bulletin board. Have the students make the spiders from black paper (yellow, orange, and white for the eyes). Display the spiders in the web.

Collecting
- Help the class gather lists of words or phrases which could be used in scary stories. Ask the students to think of:
  - scary happenings
  - scary or creepy things and noises
  - frightening places
  - good descriptive words for spooky things or happenings
  - good action words for scary stories (escape, sprang, startle)
- Have each student write at least two lists on yellow paper strips. Let the students attach their strips to the spider web.

Writing

1) Give each student a copy of the student page "The Scariest Story Ever" (page 116).
2) Instruct the students to use the words in the web to help them write a scary story about a frightening place, thing, or experience.
3) Each student should give his or her story a title that includes frightening words.

Praising

- Look for especially creepy words and phrases.
- Comment on suspenseful beginnings and interesting or surprising endings.

Polishing

- Have the students look at each sentence to see if they can replace or add "scary" words.
- Ask the students to improve their beginning sentences in order to immediately capture the reader's attention.

Showing Off

- Help the students mount their stories on black paper (or on the spiders if the spiders are large enough). Display the stories near the spider web.

The Scariest Story Ever

_____

(Title)

Write an exciting beginning sentence.

_____

_____

Write several sentences to tell what happened.

_____

_____

_____

_____

_____

_____

_____

_____

Write a good ending sentence.

_____

_____

_____

_____

28. A Horrible, Lousy Day

Materials
- Judith Viorst's book ALEXANDER AND THE TERRIBLE, HORRIBLE, NO-GOOD, VERY BAD DAY (Atheneum)
- drawing paper, construction paper, crayons, markers

Romancing
- Read the story about Alexander's horrible day to the class. (They'll enjoy it even if they've heard it before!)
- Tell the students about one of your worst days. Let the students take turns talking about awful days they've had.

Collecting
- Give each student a copy of the student page "My Most Terrible Day" (page 120).
- Instruct the students to make a list of things that happened (or could happen) on an awful day. Encourage the students to list at least six and no more than 15 ideas.
- Guide the students as they collect ideas by asking them to think about:
    - things that happened at home in the morning
    - things that happened on the way to school
    - things that happened at school
    - things that happened on the way home or after school
    - food you had to eat
    - disagreements you had with friends or family
    - things that happened at supper or after supper

  Note: Students may imagine things that might happen on a bad day and include these ideas on their lists.

Writing

Direct the students to do the following.

1) Choose eight (less for younger or less able writers) ideas from your collected lists and make sure each is written as a complete sentence.
2) Number the sentences in the best sequence.
3) Give the story a good title.
4) End the story with a line that begins "I think I'll go to _____" or with another interesting ending.

Praising

- Look for words and phrases that make an unfortunate event sound really awful.
- Comment on good sentence order that contributes to the story's interest.

Polishing

- Instruct the students to improve poor endings.
- Direct the students to vary sentence patterns and sentence length.

Showing Off

- Provide material for covers (paper, cardboard, or construction paper), crayons, and other supplies needed for each writer to make his or her story booklet.

My Most Terrible Day

Write about some things that happened to you on a bad day.

_____

_____

_____

_____

_____

_____

_____

_____

_____

_____

_____

_____

_____

(You can write more on the back.)

_____

Write the title for your "bad-day" story here.

DIVIDE THE PARAGRAPHS INTO 4-5-6 OR MORE PAGES. ILLUSTRATE EACH PAGE. ENCOURAGE STUDENTS TO USE VARIETY IN THEIR LAYOUTS. (MAKE A DUMMY BOOK FIRST.)

FRONT COVER CAN BE MADE USING LAYERS OF CONSTRUCTION PAPER.

A Pretty Bad Really Awful Day

BY Alan Bullock Grade Three

A Pretty Bad, Really Awful Day

by Alan Bullock

©1987 A.Bullock U.S.A.

TITLE PAGE

To start with, there were no Cheerios left. Then I missed the bus and was late for school.

1.

At school, our seats were all changed around. My best friend, Kenny, was absent.

2.

$2 + \frac{1}{2} = ?$ $46\overline{)7035} = ?$ ACH!

The math was too hard for me. It was so cold out that recess was cancelled.

3.

Mom was late getting home. We had chop suey for dinner, and I <u>hate</u> chop suey!

4.

The President was on T.V. so we couldn't watch anything good. I think I'll go live in a cave!

The End

5.

STAPLE PAGES INSIDE FRONT AND BACK COVERS AND DISPLAY RESULTS!

MY BAD BAD DAY

The End.

121

Example Page

29. Fortunately & Unfortunately

> The good news is that my friend gave me flowers.

> The bad news is that I'm allergic to flowers!

Materials
- white drawing paper
- extra-large drawing or construction paper (18 x 24 inches)
- crayons, markers, glue, scraps of construction paper, scissors
- FORTUNATELY, by Remy Charlip (Parents' Magazine Press)--optional

Romancing
- Read FORTUNATELY to the class, or tell them the "Good News & Bad News" story found on page 125.
- Let the students illustrate parts of the story on regular-sized drawing paper.

Collecting
- Help the students make a list of words or "happenings" for the good news of the story and a list for the bad news.
- Have the class orally create a few "fortunately-unfortunately" stories, using the starters on page 125. Each story should end with a "fortunate" statement such as "The good news is _____ ."

Writing
1) Give each student a copy of the student page "Good News & Bad News" (page 124). Students may work individually or in pairs. (You may choose to allow the students to replace the first sentence with their own beginnings.)
2) Encourage the students to use words or ideas from the lists gathered in the "collecting" step.

Praising
- Look for sentences that are clear and complete.
- Point out sentences that describe interesting, surprising, or unusual happenings.

Polishing
- Instruct the students to include a variety of sentence structures.
- Ask the students to add more colorful and more active words.

Showing Off
- Help the students make their "Good News & Bad News" stories into over-sized books using large drawing paper. (Allow several days to illustrate all of the pages.) Have the students bind and cover their books. Let the students work in small groups, or have the class make one large book. Everyone may help brainstorm for the perfect title!

But the other good news is that I have a cold and can't smell the flowers anyway!

Good News & Bad News

GOOD NEWS   Last week Tracy and Daniel went on their vacation to the beach.

BAD NEWS   _____

_____

GOOD NEWS   _____

_____

BAD NEWS   _____

_____

GOOD NEWS   _____

_____

BAD NEWS   _____

_____

GOOD NEWS   _____

_____

One day James found a huge present on his front porch.

Unfortunately, the present was wrapped very tightly with strong tape.

Fortunately, his mother gave him a sharp knife to open the package.

Unfortunately, James slit his finger with the knife.

Fortunately, a neighbor brought him a bandage.

Unfortunately, the neighbor sat on the present.

Fortunately, the package broke open.

Unfortunately, a frightened squeal came from inside the package.

Fortunately, a friendly, fluffy puppy jumped into James' arms!

Starters:

FORTUNATELY   The day of the school picnic had finally arrived.

GOOD NEWS   Michelle's grandma sent her tickets for the fair.

GOOD NEWS   Brian found out he didn't have the measles.

FORTUNATELY   The Halloween Party was ready to begin.

30. Pass It On

Romancing

- With the class sitting in a circle, begin a story as follows:

  When Jonathan visited the zoo, he always stopped to watch Godzilla, the big gorilla. One day, however, Jonathan stood too close to the cage and Godzilla was able to see the red lollipop in Jonathan's hand.
- "Pass" the story to the next person, asking him or her to add a middle to the story.
- The second person passes the story to someone else who then finishes it.
- Repeat this process with another beginning.

Collecting

- Have the class make a list of some good story starters. Write the list on the board.

Writing

1) Give each student a copy of the student page "Pass A Story" (page 127). Tell everyone to write an exciting story beginning of one or two sentences.
2) At a signal, everyone should pass his or her paper two persons to the right. Now instruct the students to add a middle to the story each has received.
3) Direct the students to pass their papers again in the same way, this time adding endings.
4) Have the students pass their papers one last time. This time each student should add a title to the paper he or she receives.

Praising

- Look for clarity in each section of the story.
- Comment on good beginnings, endings, and titles.

Polishing

- Have the students make any necessary changes to make each section (plus the title) clearer and more complete.
- Instruct the students to add more colorful or active words where needed.

Showing Off

- Read and enjoy the stories aloud.

Pass A Story

_____
title

BEGINNING _____
_____
_____
_____

MIDDLE _____
_____
_____
_____
_____
_____

ENDING _____
_____
_____
_____
_____